YOUR
HEALTHY & HAPPY
HORSE

How to Care for Your Horse & Have Fun Too!

By Lesley Ward

Nick Clemente, Special Consultant
Karla Austin, Project Manager
Michelle Martinez, Editor
Book design and layout by Bocu & Bocu
Photographs by Lesley Ward

Library of Congress Cataloging-in-Publication Data

Ward, Lesley.
  Your healthy & happy horse : how to care for your horse and have fun
too! / from the editor of Young rider magazine, Lesley Ward.
      v. cm.
Contents: Finding the right horse -- Footloose in the field -- A stable
life -- Staying healthy -- Feeding facts -- A good fit -- In and out of
the saddle -- When good horses go bad! -- Saying goodbye.
  ISBN 1-931993-40-8 (Paperback : alk. paper)
  1. Horses--Juvenile literature. 2. Horsemanship. [1. Horses. 2.
Horsemanship.] I. Title: Your healthy and happy horse. II. Title.

SF302.W343 2003
636.1'083--dc21

                           2003007070

BowTie™ Press
A Division of BowTie Inc.
3 Burroughs
Irvine, California 92618

Printed and Bound in Singapore
10 9 8 7 6 5 4 3 2 1

CONTENTS

INTRODUCTION

Galloping down leafy trails, jumping over fences, and winning ribbons at shows—these are the activities that make owning a horse lots of fun. But if you and your horse aren't well suited for each other, or if he's not looked after properly, you might not get to do any of these amazing activities.

The key to having a great time with a horse is to buy one who is right for you in the first place. Keep an open mind when you're searching. If your horse is too hot for you to handle, you won't want to spend time with him. You might want a flashy palomino, but the best horse for you might be a quiet bay.

Once you get your new partner home, it's time to think about his health and happiness. If he isn't fed properly or has to stand out in the freezing cold with no shelter, he won't feel like racing around barrels or popping over an oxer. If he's not vaccinated regularly, he might get sick and then you won't be able to ride at all.

The way you ride your horse affects his performance, too. If all you do is school in an arena every day, your horse will get bored and may lose interest in his work. If you were a horse, would you like to go around in circles all the time? Why not break up your schooling sessions and go on a trail ride with a pony pal?

Owning a horse or pony is a big responsibility. Your horse relies on you to look after him properly. If you do a good job, you'll have a super time with him—both in and out of the saddle.

Your horse is your best friend, so spend as much time with him as you can.

CHAPTER ONE

FINDING THE RIGHT HORSE

Before you begin searching for a horse, you need to ask yourself a few important questions. The first one is, "Am I experienced enough to look after a horse?" Be honest! Do you know what and how much a horse eats? Do you know what vaccinations a horse needs? Would you be able to tell if your horse was sick?

If you don't feel sure about these answers, wait a while before buying a horse. Spend as much time as you can at the barn before and after your lessons. Offer to help feed and groom the horses. Ask a pony pal if you can hang out with her and learn all you can about how she cares for her horse. It won't be long before you're ready to own a horse.

The second question you must ask yourself is, "What kind of horse do I need?" Young riders often buy unsuitable horses, and then no one wins. The horses end up being ridden by trainers or sold—and who knows what fate awaits them then? Life would be better for many horses if their riders had spent a little more time searching for suitable four-legged partners.

While you can't guarantee that the horse you buy is going to be perfect—very few horses are—you can take some sensible steps that will increase your chance of finding a good partner, one that will have a happy home with you for a long time.

STARTING YOUR SEARCH

The key to buying a suitable four-legged partner is finding one that can do the activities you want to do. Never force a horse to do a job he can't do; he'll end up unhappy and frustrated. If you want to barrel race, there's no point in buying a dressage star. If you want to compete in pleasure classes, don't buy a speedy horse. If you want to trail ride, don't buy a hyperactive horse.

Left: *A slow, steady horse can do great in western pleasure classes.*
Above: *Offer to groom the pony you ride at riding school.*

Before you begin your search, sit down with your parents and make a list of the things you want to do with your horse. Here are some fun equestrian activities:

- Barrel racing
- Competitive or noncompetitive trail riding
- Cutting
- Dressage
- Endurance riding
- Eventing
- Gymkhana events and mounted games
- Jumping
- Reining

When you meet a horse for the first time, tell his owners what activities you'd like to do with him. If they want their horse to go to a good home, they'll be honest and let you know what he can and can't do.

WHERE TO LOOK

Start your search by letting your pony pals know that you're looking for a horse. Call up local Pony Club and 4-H leaders. They might know of a horse who needs a new rider. If you have a trainer, she should be able to line up some horses for you to try. Go to the local tack shop and look at the bulletin board where people post pictures and details about horses they are selling. Some of the best horses don't get advertised—they sell by word of mouth. It's great to learn about a local horse who's

for sale because then it's easier to find out more about him.

Also, look in the newspaper and check the "Horses for Sale" section in the classifieds. Hunt for ads that contain phrases such as, "perfect kid's horse," "quiet and calm," and "good to clip and trailer." Avoid ads with phrases such as, "green horse" or "needs experienced rider."

Don't shop for your horse at an auction. Unless it's a big sale organized by a breed association, buying a horse at an auction is too risky. You can't try the horse properly and you won't know anything about his background.

Left: Do you want to compete in show jumping classes with your horse?
Above: This is one of the fun things you can do at a Gymkhana event.

PERSONALITY PLUS

You want a horse who is good-tempered and friendly. It's almost impossible to change a horse's personality as he gets older, so don't think that you'll be able to make a grouchy horse nicer. He shouldn't make grumpy faces or fidget when you handle him. Avoid buying a horse who's stubborn, high-strung, or nervous. Stay away from bullies who push you around in the stable. Even if a horse can jump five-foot fences, you won't enjoy owning him if he bites or kicks.

YOUNG HORSES AND YOUNG RIDERS

It's not usually a good idea to buy a young horse—especially if you're learning how to ride. Most horses need several years of training before they become quiet and reliable. For your first horse, it's better to buy an older, more experienced mount.

If you fall in love with a horse who is less than three years old, you must have a trainer or knowledgeable adult help you work with him. A young horse can pick up bad habits like bucking or dropping his head to eat grass. Horses are big, unpredictable animals, and they can take advantage of kids.

On the other hand, you can start having fun with an older horse right away. You won't have to wait several years before competing or jumping. Horses can live into their twenties, so a "teenager" will probably be around for a long time.

WHICH BREED IS BEST?

Keep an open mind about what breed of horse you'd like. You might think quarter horses are just for western riding, but they can do all sorts of activities, including dressage, jumping, and eventing. Arabians are great at endurance riding, but they also can be dressage stars. If you like a particular breed, go to that breed's Web site and learn more about it.

If you're looking for a first horse, consider a mixed breed—sometimes called a "grade" horse. Some of the best horses are mixed breeds because they tend to be hardier than purebred horses, have fewer health problems, and are often quieter than their registered cousins.

MARE OR GELDING?

If you find a horse you like, it doesn't matter if that horse is a gelding (neutered male) or a mare (female). Both sexes can make excellent horses for young riders, although some mares can be moody and sensitive when they are "in season" (ready to mate). But this grouchy behavior lasts only a few days a month in the spring and summer. Stallions are not suitable for young riders because they can be unpredictable in their behavior. Besides, stallions are not allowed at 4-H and Pony Club events.

HOW BIG?

The size of your horse is important. A horse who is too big for you will cause problems.

You must be able to tack up your horse by yourself.

You won't be strong enough to control him, and your legs won't be long enough to give him the correct aids if he misbehaves. (Your legs must reach at least halfway down his sides.) You also must be able to tack up your horse on your own. If he is so tall that you cannot put on the saddle or get the bridle over his ears, he's not the horse for you. In addition, you must be able to get on your horse without a mounting block. Why? Because there probably won't be a mounting block handy if you fall off on a trail ride! If you're too big for a horse, you likely won't keep him long enough to develop a good relationship. Remember—you're going to grow, too.

TRYING A HORSE

When you meet a horse for the first time, ask if you can help groom and tack him up. Watch how he behaves when he's being handled. By spending time with him before you ride, you'll get to know him a bit better. If he turns away from you or puts his ears back, he might not be the right horse for a kid. Check out his tack. A quiet, well-behaved horse will probably wear a simple snaffle and a plain noseband. If he's wearing a severe bit like a three-ring gag or a figure-eight noseband, he might be too strong for you.

Ask someone else to ride the horse before you do. Watch as she mounts and rides him around the arena. Does he look obedient and fun to ride? If so, hop on and

have a go. Perform all the activities that you might ask him to do at home. Canter in circles, pop over a few fences, and go for a walk around the barn area. If the owner will let you ride him a second time, do it. The more you ride your potential horse, the better. After riding him a couple of times, you'll probably know if he's the right horse for you. You should feel comfortable and happy riding him. If you feel scared, don't buy him. You'll eventually find a horse who's right for you.

Above: *A quiet horse wears a simple snaffle bit.*
Right: *Pop over a fence or two when trying a pony.*

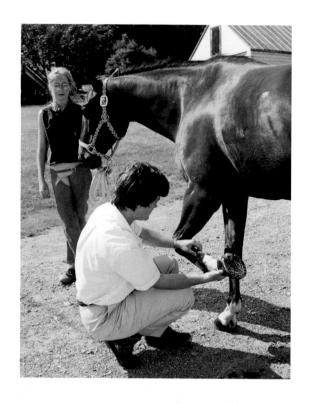

When you decide to buy a horse, a veterinarian should give him a pre-purchase exam. That way, you won't get him home only to find he's got an old leg injury and won't be able to jump.

MOVING DAY

Moving is stressful for a horse. Don't ride him the first day he arrives at his new home. He may act nervous and silly, and you'll get frustrated. It will take him a few weeks to get used to his new surroundings. In fact, you should wait at least a week before riding him. During that first week, take him for walks around the barn on a lead rope and let him graze. Grooming and handling him will help you learn about his personality and let him get to know you.

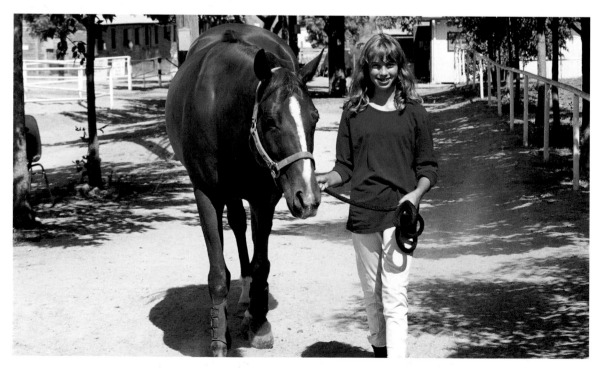

FIRST RIDE

Once your horse has settled into his new home, you can saddle him up. It takes awhile to get used to a new horse, so try not to get annoyed if his behavior isn't good or if your rides aren't 100 percent perfect. If you're patient, within a few weeks, you'll know your horse well and the real fun will begin.

When you ride for the first time, it's best to avoid galloping along the trails near the barn. Instead, stick to the arena. See how he gets along with other horses. Pop over a fence or two. Relax and get to know each other.

When you do go out on a trail for the first time, follow a friend who's riding a well-behaved horse. Since you don't know how your horse will act, it's a good idea to have someone along who can help if you run into problems.

Left Top: *A vet should examine a horse before you buy him.*
Left Bottom: *Take your horse for walks around his new barn.*
Above: *Stay in the arena for your first few rides.*

19

LOTS OF LESSONS

If possible, sign up for regular lessons with a good instructor. Without lessons, we can get a bit lazy and repeat the same exercises over and over again. Even Olympic riders take lessons. Schooling your horse in the arena can be dull, and it's often hard to think of different drills. An instructor will help you create a variety of exercises so you and your horse won't get bored. And, if you're having problems with your horse, an experienced person on the ground can help you work them out.

Left: *Take a friend along on your first trail ride.*
Above: *Sign up for regular lessons with your new horse.*

CHAPTER TWO

FOOTLOOSE IN THE FIELD

If you're lucky enough to keep your horse at a barn with a big field, make sure she's out in it as much as possible. Just as you wouldn't like to be locked in your room all day, neither would your horse. Keeping your horse cooped up in a stall twenty-four hours a day is bad for her mental and physical health. Horses like to roam and graze outside. It's no wonder that stabled horses develop frustrating habits like weaving or cribbing. Horses are meant to be outside, moving around, and nibbling on grass all day long—just like they do in the wild.

PONY PALS

Does your horse live in a field with other horses? If she doesn't, she should. A horse who lives by herself can get depressed because horses don't like being alone. After all, in the wild, they run in herds. How big of a field does your horse need? That will depend on the number of horses you have. There should be at least one acre per horse. If a field has too many horses in it, the good grass will get munched down and the horses will have too little to eat. The grass that's left will become covered in manure and eventu-ally stop growing. Then your horse would be stuck in a field with nasty-tasting weeds and no nutritious grass.

To make sure a field is a peaceful place to live, it's best to place feed buckets far apart so that each horse has plenty of space while eating. Try to feed every horse the same amount of food so one doesn't finish early and push another horse off her food. If there are five horses in a field, put out six piles of hay. If one horse gets pushed off her pile of hay, there will be a free one for her to go to.

Left: A horse can nibble on grass all day long.
Above: Horses are happiest when they live in a herd.

Most horses get along out in the field. They're more interested in eating grass than fighting. Horses who are friends stick close to each other. They graze side by side and stand head to tail and swish flies off each other's faces. If they feel itchy, they might mutually groom each other by nibbling on each other's withers.

One horse is usually the boss, and the others must obey her. The top banana gets fed first and will sometimes chase her field mates away from hay or feed. Unfortunately, there is usually a horse at the bottom of the ladder. She gets fed last, and gets bossed around by the other horses. If a horse has been in a pasture for a while, she usually figures out where her place is in the group, and everyone gets along fine.

NEW KID ON THE BLOCK

When bringing your new horse to a barn, there are ways to help her become accepted into the group of horses. Being the new horse in the barn is scary. She doesn't know any of the other horses or how they will behave toward her. Don't just lead the new horse out into the field the minute she gets off the trailer. You'll be asking for trouble. The new horse might get kicked or hurt by the other horses.

If you can, put your horse in a field next to the established herd for a few days. All the horses will spend lots of time sniffing each other over the fence, and there might even be some silly squealing and snorting. A good time to turn a new horse out into a field is while the other horses are eating. If they're like most horses, they'll pay more attention to their food than to any new horse.

Before turning her out, deworm your horse in case she's got parasites. Then turn her out in a leather halter. Never use a nylon halter because it could get caught on something. If this happens, the nylon halter won't break and your horse could get strangled.

While the other horses are munching, your horse will have a chance to walk or trot around a bit and get to know her new home. Then, one by one, you'll notice the other horses lifting up their heads to check out the new horse. Stay outside the field and watch as the herd meets your horse. At first, there will be lots of sniffing between them. Then for a while, they will run around like loonies. It might look like the others are ganging up on your horse, but it's best to leave them alone. After about 20 minutes, the horses will probably put their heads down and start eating again.

It may take a few weeks for your horse to settle completely into her new home. She'll have to figure out where she fits into

the group. She may even get into a few scuffles with other horses and end up with a few cuts and scrapes. Be patient—it won't be long before she's nibbling on another horse's withers.

Left: *Horses often scratch each other's itchy parts.*
Above: *Turn out your horse in a leather halter.*

FIELD CARE

It's your responsibility to make sure your horse's field is a safe and healthy place for her to live. Here are some things to consider:

Fencing: The field should have a strong fence without gaps or broken parts. A wooden plank fence or a horse-safe mesh fence is best. Don't put your horse in a field with a barbed wire fence. Barbed wire is extremely dangerous and can leave scars if your horse should get caught in it.

Water: The field should have a steady supply of clean, fresh tap water. Water should be kept in a rubber or metal trough, or you can use an automatic waterer. A stream or pond is not a good source of clean water. Both can be dangerous to you and your horse if they should ice over in the winter. Your horse can die if she falls into icy cold water.

Shelter: Your horse needs a place in the field where she can get out of the cold wind in the winter, or be in some shade in the summer. Ideally, the field will have a run-in shed, a three-sided wooden building that your horse can walk into and out of as she likes. If there's no shelter, the field should have trees to help protect your horse from the elements. What if there aren't any trees or shelter? You should find a different place for your horse to board—one that has a barn where she can go when the weather is severe.

Left: *A wooden plank fence is quite safe.*
Above: *Your horse appreciates a run-in shelter in her field.*

27

REGULAR JOBS

If your horse lives in a field, here are some jobs you must do on a regular basis to make sure she stays safe in her grassy home:

Every Day Jobs: Visit your horse every single day to make sure she's okay. Look her over from head to tail and pick out her hooves. Check that her water trough is full. In the summer, a horse can drink more than 15 gallons of water a day. Clean the trough by removing leaves or other debris.

Once a Week Jobs: Grab a pitchfork and a wheelbarrow. Then go out in the field and pick up piles of poop. This is an important chore because horses are fussy eaters and won't eat grass that has manure on it. Manure also ruins the grass underneath it. In addition, piles of manure attract pesky flies in the summer and make great homes for worm eggs. After collecting the manure, dump it on a muckheap.

Top: *Remove piles of manure every week.*
Bottom: *Check the water trough every day.*

Walk around the field and pick up any garbage that has blown into the field. Plastic bags and cans can be dangerous if a horse gets a hold of them. Also check the fence line. If a board is loose, grab a hammer and nail and fix it yourself or ask your parents or the barn owner to take care of it. If there's a loose plank, a horse is bound to find it. Horses seem to look for trouble!

PIPE CORRALS

Some parts of the country may not have grassy fields, so horses live in pipe corrals or pens. If your horse is going to live in a corral, make sure she has plenty of room to move around and lie down. A corral for one horse should be no smaller than 12 feet by 24 feet. It should have some sort of shelter because your horse needs to take cover from rain or extreme heat.

Top: *Fix loose fence boards right away.*
Bottom: *Pick up trash that has blown into the field.*

Most corrals have dirt or sand on the ground. You need to muck out the corral every single day or it will get dirty and be an unpleasant place for your horse to live. Plus, your horse will be covered in manure and urine stains. Even if you board at a barn where mucking out is done for you, check the corral every day. You may need to do additional mucking out yourself.

You need to replace the bedding in the corral on a regular basis by adding more sand or dirt. There are also special absorbent bedding materials available at feed stores. If your horse doesn't have enough bedding in her corral, she may get sores on her hocks that can take a long time to heal.

If your horse lives at a boarding barn with pipe corrals, try to get her placed in a corral beside a nice horse. It can be stressful if the horse next door is always lunging at or trying to bite your horse. In the field, horses have room to move away from each other, but in a corral, your horse can't move away from the horse next door. You may have to move your horse several times before she finds friendly neighbors.

Left: *Pipe corrals should be partially covered.*
Above: *Muck out your horse's corral every day.*

CHAPTER THREE

A STABLE LIFE

Most horses are happiest if they're left outside—especially if they're hardy mixed breeds with shaggy coats, and they have plenty of food and hay available. But if you live in an area that gets chilly in the winter, your horse may have to be stabled at night. A horse with a thin coat like a Thoroughbred or an Arabian may get cold in nippy temperatures and could get sick or lose weight trying to keep warm.

Some horses stay inside their stalls' during the day in the summer months, too. If pesky flies torment your horse, or if there's no shade in his field, you may have to bring him inside for a few hours each day. But if these conditions don't exist, and you have the choice between stabling him or leaving him in a field with shelter in it, let him stay outside during the summer. He'll be happier in his field and you can always cover him with a lightweight fly sheet if he's bothered by bugs.

LET ME OUT!

There are big boarding barns in places such as Southern California, where horses stay in their stalls all the time because there are no fields nearby. If you keep your horse at such a barn or ranch, consider moving him to a place where there are pipe corrals with shelters or in-and-outs (a stall that has a pen or corral attached to it).

Living inside 24 hours a day is an unnatural lifestyle for a horse. It's not good for his legs, his mind, or his digestive system. Horses who live indoors suffer more colic attacks and develop more vices than horses who live outdoors. If you have no choice but to keep your horse in a stall all the time, try to lease a stall that gives him a good view of all the barn activities—one that looks outside instead of into the middle aisle of the barn.

Left: *A stable can be a pretty boring place for a horse.*
Above: *A stabled horse needs lots of turn out time.*

Be sure to hand walk your horse every day. Lead him around the barn and let him nibble on patches of grass. Also, you must get to the barn once or twice a day and let him spend some time in a turnout arena. When you get him outside, don't chase him around at top speed—this can cause leg problems because he won't be warmed up properly. Instead, let him wander around and roll if he wants. This is his turnout time so let him do as he pleases. In other words, get him out of his stall as much as you can.

THE STALL

Your horse's stall must be big enough for him to walk around in and lie down. If you're checking out a boarding barn, take along a tape measure and measure the stall. A stall that measures 12 feet by 10 feet is okay for a pony up to 14.2hh, but a horse needs an area 12 feet by 12 feet or more. If you have a mare who's ready to foal, you need an even bigger stall—at least 14 feet by 16 feet. Also, the ceiling must be at least 10 feet from the ground so your horse won't bump his head if he rears.

The stall must have a large door, at least 4 feet wide and 8 feet tall, so both you and your horse have plenty of room to pass through. All stall doors should open outward. The best stall doors are divided in half horizontally so the bottom can be closed, leaving the top open for your horse to stick his head through.

Some people think it's unsafe for a horse to stick out his head because he might bite someone. If your horse is likely to bite, cover the doorway with a mesh panel or place a metal grid over the top half. If your horse is well behaved and doesn't bite, go ahead and let him stick out his head to see what's going on.

Left: *Get your horse out of the stable and let him graze.*
Above: *Horses like to see what's going on around the barn.*

Always have two bolts on the lower door—one at the top and one at the bottom. If you have a clever horse who can manage to undo the top bolt, at least he won't be able to reach the bottom one. After all, you don't want him escaping and causing chaos!

The walls of the stall should be strong and solid, which will keep the horse in the next stall from biting or touching your horse. Some stalls have wood from the floor to the middle of the wall, and then a grill or mesh from the middle to the ceiling. This is fine if the neighboring horses get along. If they don't, they may spend a lot of time kicking or lunging at each other

and this can be stressful on both horses.

It's nice if the stall has a window to let in light and fresh air. You should make sure the glass is protected with strong wire mesh or bars so your horse can't break through. Check to see if the stall has a light. You'll need one if you have to groom or handle your horse at night. The light should be covered and out of your horse's reach.

The stall should have one or two horse-safe hooks for hanging water and feed buckets. And, there should be a safe place to put hay. If the stall has a hayrack, check that it doesn't have sharp edges that could cut your horse.

BEDDING

If you want your horse to be comfortable in his stall, cover the floor with a thick layer (at least one foot) of soft bedding. Don't skimp on bedding! Standing on hard cement or a dirt floor can cause your horse to have lameness or painful hock sores that take a long time to heal. Also, deep bedding cuts down on drafts in the stall and keeps your horse warm if he lies down.

To make sure you've got enough bedding, try this easy test: stick a pitchfork in the bedding. You shouldn't be able to feel the ground. Another thing you can do is lie down on it yourself (if it's clean). If you're comfy, your horse will be comfy, too. Even if there are rubber mats on the floor of the barn, the stall still needs bedding to keep your horse warm and to absorb urine. Here are the two most common types of bedding you'll find at local feed stores:

Wood Shavings: If you own a gray horse, wood shavings are the best bedding for him. They are easy to pick clean and your horse won't get as visibly dirty as he would if he had straw in his stall. A deep bed of four or five sacks of shavings will make a comfortable place for your horse to lie on.

Straw: A pile of about four bales of straw makes a comfortable and warm bed for your horse. Make sure the bales are thoroughly dry. Wet straw gets moldy, which can make your horse sick. Also,

straw gets dirty quickly, so muck out the stall regularly.

MUCKING OUT

Walk into a dirty stall and take a whiff. You wouldn't want to be stuck in there, would you? Neither does your horse! You must muck out his stall once or twice *every single day*. A dirty stall is unhygienic and the smell of ammonia caused by your horse's urine can burn his lungs and make it hard for him to breathe. A stall that isn't cleaned regularly will also result in a dirty horse and dirty blankets.

Left: *Always make sure the door bolts are fastened.*
Above: *Shavings and straw are the most popular bedding materials.*

It's not a great idea to muck out while your horse is in the stall, because you might poke him with a pitchfork or he might escape out the open door. Turn him out in his field before you get to work. If you muck out in the morning, remove all wet patches and manure, then sweep or rake the remaining bedding out from the center and close to the walls. Leave the middle of the floor and any other wet patches to dry for a few hours. If your horse has urinated in the stall, sprinkle around some lime powder to deodorize the area. Lime powder is a strong substance, so wear rubber gloves when you handle it—and it wouldn't hurt to cover your mouth and nose with a bandana so you don't inhale any powder. You can buy lime powder at an agricultural supply store. Dump the manure on a muckheap, which should be located far away from the barn. Muckheaps attract flies, which you don't want near the horses.

When you return to the stall in the afternoon, rake the old bedding into the middle again and add lots of new bedding. Always bank up the bedding (make it higher) around the stable walls. Why? Banking prevents your horse from lying too close to the

Above Left: *Turn out your horse before you begin mucking out.*
Above Middle: *Remove all wet patches and manure.*
Above Right: *Dump the muck on a heap far away from the barn.*

wall and getting cast (stuck), which is a serious problem for your horse and scary for him, too. If this happens, it may take several strong adults to pull your horse away from the wall so he can get up again.

A CLEAN SWEEP

There are other things you can do to make your horse's stall a pleasant place. For instance, scrub out his buckets at least once a week to keep them free from bacteria. Give the barn a good sweep every few weeks to get rid of cobwebs. This cuts down on dust and helps your horse breathe in fresh air. Cobwebs can also be fire hazards since they burn easily.

GOOD NIGHT

If your horse lives at your house, always check on him in his stall one last time before going to bed. Make sure he has enough water and hay to last him until the morning. If you have a pitchfork handy, pick up any droppings and put them in a muck bucket. Doing this helps to keep his blankets cleaner. Your horse might also like an apple (cut up into easy-to-chew quarters) as a bedtime treat.

Above Left: *Don't be stingy with bedding!*
Above Middle: *Scrub out buckets regularly.*
Above Right: *Grab a brush to sweep away cobwebs.*

CHAPTER FOUR

STAYING HEALTHY

It doesn't matter if your horse lives in your backyard or at a boarding barn—you must visit her every day to make sure she's healthy. If she's out in a field, walk out to her to look her over. You should know the signs of good health in your horse. You don't have to be a vet to tell if she's sick. If you spend lots of time with her, you'll see when she's limping, acting differently, or not eating her food.

If you have to go away, ask a friend experienced in caring for horses to check on her while you're gone. Post your veterinarian's name and number near the stall, in case your horse becomes injured or ill. If you live on a farm, explain the signs of a sick horse to your neighbors. Show them where your veterinarian's number is posted. If they spot your horse acting strangely when you're not at home, they can call the vet.

A HEALTHY HORSE:
- is alert and interested in everything that's going on around her;
- moves around her field and nibbles on grass or hay;
- eats all her food;
- has a shiny coat;
- has legs and hooves that are cool to the touch;
- puts weight on all four feet;
- has manure that is firm and ball-shaped.

Left: *A healthy horse gobbles up all of her food.*
Above: *Visit your horse out in the field every day.*

A SICK HORSE:

- looks depressed and hangs her head low;
- doesn't move around;
- doesn't eat her food;
- doesn't drink water;
- limps or drags a foot;
- coughs or has an extremely runny nose and runny eyes;
- has runny droppings;
- has a dull coat and bare patches;
- nips or looks at her stomach, rolls violently, or acts like she needs to urinate but doesn't. These are signs of colic—a serious stomachache that can kill a horse.

FIRST AID KIT

Keep a first aid kit at the barn at all times. The following items should be in your kit:
- Clean sponges
- Cotton pads or gauze squares
- Disinfectant or antiseptic solution— for cleaning cuts
- Duct tape—to secure bandages in place
- Epsom salts—for soaking sore hooves
- Saline solution—to clean dirt out of wounds
- Scissors
- Several different sizes of stretch bandages
- Veterinary thermometer
- Wound powder or spray

If a wound is small, you may be able to treat it yourself. Simply dip a wad of cotton or gauze in clean water and wipe the wound clean. Apply first aid powder or spray to the wound. Don't put a bandage on a small wound; it will heal more quickly if left uncovered.

If a wound is bleeding badly, it's serious. Grab a cotton pad and press it on the wound. As you apply pressure, shout for someone to call the vet. If the wound is on a leg, you may be able to keep the pad in place by wrapping a stretchy bandage around the cotton and securing it with duct tape.

Remember to replace items that you use from your first aid kit so the kit is always fully stocked.

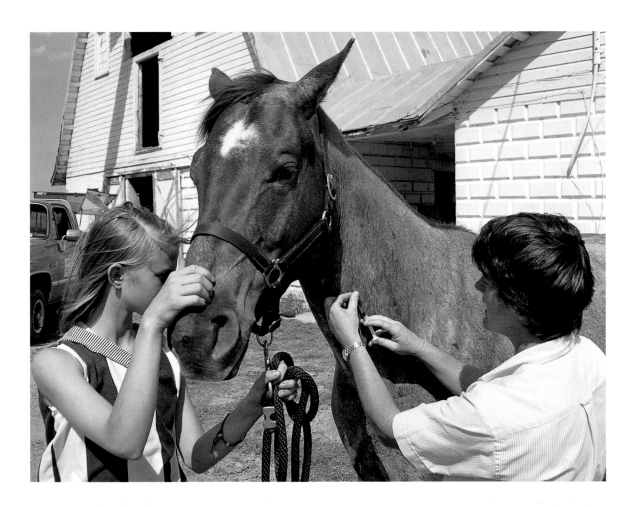

REGULAR VETERINARY CHECKUPS

When looking for a vet, you should find one who is experienced, good with horses, and who is happy to answer your questions. Also, try to find a local vet who can get to your barn quickly in case of an emergency.

If your horse is in good health you're lucky, because the veterinarian will need to visit your horse only once or twice a year.

The main visit is for yearly vaccinations. If you plan to go to shows or trail ride, your horse will need the vaccinations appropriate for your area. Most likely, the veterinarian will vaccinate your horse for:

- Encephalomyelitis (sleeping sickness)
- Influenza (flu)
- Rabies
- Tetanus (lockjaw)
- West Nile Virus

Left: Make sure you have a first aid kit at the barn.
Above: A vet must vaccinate your horse every year.

OPEN WIDE

Your horse needs her teeth floated (rasped) at least once a year—maybe more often if she's very young or old. Teeth that are too long or sharp can hurt your horse and prevent her from eating properly. You'll know that her teeth need floating if lots of food is falling out of her mouth and onto the ground when she eats. Veterinarians can float teeth, but horse dentists are available, too. When this procedure is needed, the veterinarian or dentist puts a device called a speculum in your horse's mouth to keep it open, and then floats the teeth with a big metal file.

WIGGLY WORMS

Worms are another potential problem that needs regular care. It's hard to put weight on a wormy horse and she can also get colicky from them. Therefore, you must deworm your horse every two months so parasites don't damage her blood vessels, intestines, lungs, and heart.

Dewormers are sold at tack or feed stores; ask your veterinarian which one to use. Most horse owners rotate between different types of dewormers so the parasites don't become immune to one type. The amount you give your horse depends on her weight. To figure this out, wrap a

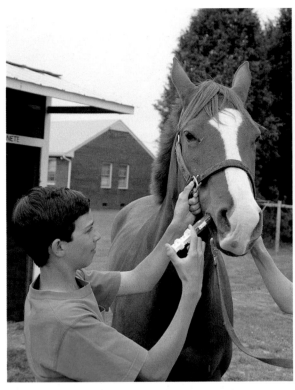 

weight tape measure around her belly. This will tell you how much she weighs.

If there are several horses boarding in the same field, deworm all of them at the same time. If you deworm your horse but not the others, the dewormer will have almost no effect because she'll be munching on grass covered in worms left by the other horses' manure.

FEET FIRST

A horse's hooves are like human nails. They grow about a quarter of an inch a month, so they need to be trimmed and filed (rasped) into shape every four to six weeks. This is usually done by a farrier. When looking for a farrier, try to find one who is calm and patient. If your horse squirms during the procedure and the farrier yells at or hits her, you should look for another farrier. If your horse's hooves get too long, they may crack or break off and she may become sore or lame.

Many riding horses wear shoes. These protect the hooves from the hard ground and rocks, and they also prevent the hooves from wearing down. If your horse isn't ridden on hard surfaces, she may not need shoes, but her hooves still need to be trimmed regularly.

Left: An equine dentist must float your horse's teeth at least once a year.
Above Left: Deworm your horse every 6-8 weeks.
Above Right: A farrier must trim your horse's hooves every 4-6 weeks.

GROOMING

Regular grooming has lots of benefits. It not only cleans your horse but it also improves her circulation because being brushed is invigorating. In addition, it brings the skin's natural oils to the surface, which makes her coat shine. Always groom your horse before riding her since mud can cause rubs under the saddle or bridle. Be gentle when you groom her and use soft brushes. Some horses are ticklish and don't like the feel of a rubber or plastic currycomb. Metal currycombs are scratchy and should be used only to clean other brushes. After you ride, groom your horse again to remove sweat and dust.

THAT FEELS GOOD!

Keeping your horse healthy requires more than vet checkups and grooming. Here are a few therapies your horse might appreciate on a regular basis:

Chiropractic: Does your horse flinch when you hop in the saddle? Does she refuse to jump? She may have a back problem that's affecting her performance. Equine chiropractors believe that a misalignment of the spine causes many problems—some of the individual vertebrae (bones in the back) that make up the spine may be out of place. If this is the case, her nerves are pinched, which causes her pain.

A chiropractor realigns your horse's spinal column by making short, thrusting movements to her vertebrae starting at her head and neck and moving down to her tail. Moving your horse's spine into the correct position helps the nerves in and around it work properly. Most horses seem to like the chiropractor working on them.

Massage Therapy: If your horse feels stiff or sore after jumping a tough cross-country course, sometimes a massage can make her feel better. Ask your vet to recommend an experienced massage therapist, who can firmly stroke the muscles of your horse's neck, back, hips, and thighs with her hands. Massage relaxes the muscles and encourages blood to circulate in them. If your horse is constantly sore, have a veterinarian take a look at her. The soreness may be caused by a poorly fitting saddle or by bad riding, in which case, a massage probably won't solve the problem.

Stretches: When you're about to engage in strenuous activity, such as taking a gymnastics class or running on the track, you must stretch before you start. Stretching is a great way to prevent injuries because it gets your body ready for exercise. Your horse can benefit from stretching, too.

Stretching lubricates your horse's joints, sharpens her reflexes, and releases fluids that have built up in her muscles when she hasn't been worked for a while. Stretching can make your horse more supple, too. Be

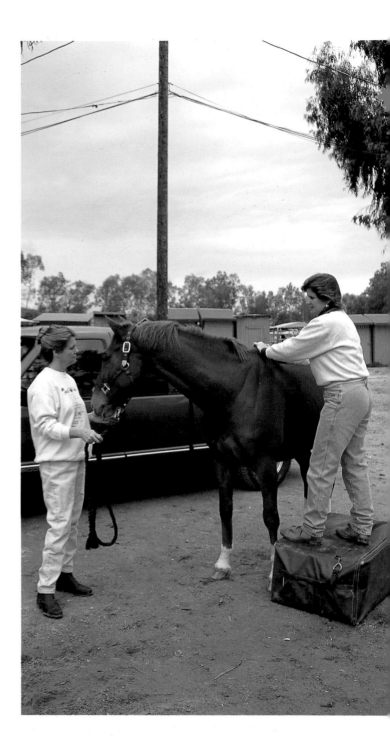

Left: *Being brushed makes your pony feel good.*
Above: *A chiropractor works on your horse's spine.*

47

gentle when you're stretching your horse. If she seems uncomfortable, stop immediately and ask a veterinarian to check her out. Here are four stretches you can do with your horse before you ride:

- **Neck Stretches:** Stand next to your horse and hold a treat near her girth area. She should stretch her head and neck around toward you until she can nibble the treat. Let her move her head back into its normal position. Then do it again. Repeat this three times on each side, lengthening the stretch each time.

- **Hoof Circles:** Pick up your horse's front hoof as if you're going to pick it out. Move it around in a circular motion for

about ten seconds. This exercise loosens up your horse's leg and shoulder. Then repeat with the other hoof.

Top: *Move her hooves around in a circular motion.*
Bottom: *Neck stretches make your horse more supple.*

- **Front Leg Stretch:** Grasp your horse's lower leg below the knee and stretch the leg forward. Hold the stretch for two or three seconds. Then place the leg gently back on the ground. Do this several times and then repeat on the other front leg.
- **Tail Whirls:** Gently grasp the tail around the dock area (close to the bony end of the tail) and lean back slightly while gently rocking the tail from side to side. This exercise loosens up your horse's back. Do this exercise four or five times.

Top: *Stretch out your horse's forelegs.*
Bottom: *Gently rock her tail back from side to side.*

CHAPTER FIVE

FEEDING YOUR HORSE

A wild horse nibbles on grass all day long because a horse's digestive system works best if he's constantly munching. High-quality grass is the perfect food for a horse because it's full of the vitamins and nutrients he needs to stay healthy. Domesticated horses don't always have access to the green stuff. In fact, some horses live in pens or stalls and don't get to eat grass at all. And, because we make them jump fences, go trail riding, and gallop around barrels, our horses need to eat grain and hay so they have plenty of energy for these activities.

If your horse gets the correct amount of food every day, and drinks plenty of water, he'll have a shiny coat and be able to do the work you ask him to do. If he doesn't get enough food and water, he'll be thin and scruffy and run out of gas when you ask him to jump or gallop.

To learn more about different kinds of feed, go to a feed store and read some of the sack labels. Most feed companies have Web

Left: *Eating grass keeps your horse's digestive system working properly.*
Above: *Your horse needs food to give him energy to run and jump.*

NEW HORSE

Before your new horse arrives at your barn, find out what kind of feed and hay he eats and have some ready. Keeping his diet the same will make his move less stressful and he'll also be less likely to suffer an equine stomachache. If you want to change his feed, wait a few weeks until he's settled in and then gradually introduce a new type of food. To introduce new food, see Feeding Rule #9 below.

FEEDING RULES

Here are the ten golden rules of feeding. Follow them religiously and your horse's digestive system will thank you.

1. Fresh water

Your horse must have an unlimited supply of fresh water. (He can drink 10-18 gallons on a hot summer day.) If a horse doesn't get enough water, he can get dehydrated and sick.

2. Feed little and often

Giving your horse one big meal a day can cause digestive problems because horses have tiny stomachs. So, it's best to feed him small amounts of food several times a day. Three meals a day is best, but if you can't feed him at lunchtime, then feeding him twice a day is fine. If your horse is in a stall or a pen all day, give him hay to munch on.

sites that tell you what kind of feed would be suitable for your horse. Find out what your friends feed their horses, too.

If you keep your horse at a boarding barn, you might not have control over what he eats. At some barns, all the horses are given the same feed. Talk to the barn manager about your horse's feeding requirements. A caring manager will try to make sure your horse gets the food he needs. If you want to give him a supplement or extra feed, you may have to visit him on a daily basis and give it to him yourself. This shouldn't be a problem—you should visit your horse every day, anyway.

Top: If your horse lives at a big barn, you may have to give him extra feed yourself.
Right: A horse must have an unlimited source of water to drink.

3. Feed around the same time each day

Horses are happiest if they have a regular mealtime. You don't have to feed them at exactly the same time every, single day, but try to keep your horse's feeding time within an hour or so each day.

4. Feed lots of fiber

Horses need to eat lots of roughage (fiber) to keep their digestive systems working properly. Fiber comes from foods like hay and grass. If your horse is penned or stabled, make sure he has plenty of hay, or feed him hay cubes.

5. Feed fresh, high-quality food

Check sack labels to make sure you are using food that has not reached its expiration date. (If a newly-opened sack of feed smells weird, take it back to the shop.) Feed should be stored in metal or plastic garbage cans, and hay should be placed on pallets and stored in a dry place because wet hay gets moldy and can make a horse sick.

6. Feed succulents

Succulents are juicy foods like apples and carrots. Your horse will like these treats and they are good for his digestive system.

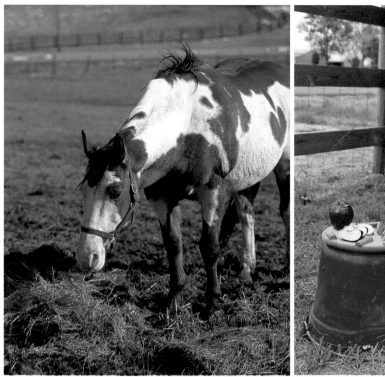

Above Left: Hay is a great source of fiber.
Above Right: Add juicy foods like apples and carrots to your horse's diet.
Right: Put a salt block in your horse's field.

7. Season with salt

Put a salt block in your horse's stall or out in his field. Salt is an essential mineral and a horse loses it when he sweats. Having a salt block to lick whenever he wants helps him replenish his salt levels.

8. Feed according to need

The amount of food your horse eats depends on his age, size, breed, and how much work he does. For example, a race-horse shouldn't get fed the same amount as a pony. If you need help figuring out how much food your horse needs, go to a feed store and read the different feed sacks. Most have guides to help you estimate how much food to give to your horse. You can find out approximately how much your horse weighs by using a weight tape.

9. Make diet changes gradually

Horses have sensitive stomachs and a sudden change in feed can give them colic. Mix the old food with the new food for about a week, increasing the new food and decreasing the old food on a daily basis. The same process applies to hay: If you change his hay, mix the new hay in with the old for a few days, switching over gradually.

Be careful if you move your horse from a bare field to one with lots of grass. Eating too much grass can cause laminitis (founder), a serious blood disease that makes a horse lame. Let him graze for only a few hours every day, slowly increasing the time he spends in the new field.

10. Wait an hour after feeding to exercise

A horse needs time to digest a meal properly, so wait about an hour before exercising him. It's hard for him to work when he's got a pound of grain in his stomach.

TYPES OF FEED

There are two main types of horse feed: roughage and concentrates. Roughage, which keeps your horse's digestive system working smoothly, is grass, hay, hay cubes, or hay pellets. Most horses get their roughage from hay—grass that has been cut in the summer and stored in bales. All horses need lots of roughage. In fact, if your horse doesn't do much work, he may be able to thrive on a diet of high-quality hay. The following are several types of hay:

- **Grass hay:** a low-energy and filling hay made from a variety of grasses.
- **Alfalfa hay:** a high-energy, protein-rich hay suitable for thin horses or those doing a lot of work.
- **Timothy hay:** a stalky, low-energy hay.

If you buy hay, check that it's fresh by opening a bale and giving it a sniff. It should smell sweet. If it is dusty or smells bad, don't feed it to your horse. Also examine the color—it should look greenish-yellow.

Concentrated feeds are grain, mixed feeds, and pellets, such as oats, corn, barley, and bran. Some horse owners mix grains to make their own feeds, but you're better off buying complete feeds that come in a sack. Usually this type of feed has been developed by an equine nutritionist. It is made by crushing together several different types of chopped-up grain to create sweet feeds or pellets. They contain all of the vitamins and minerals that your horse needs. Complete feeds are available especially for pregnant mares, foals, horses in training, fat horses, thin horses, and old horses.

SUPPLEMENTS

Most complete feeds contain all the nutrients your horse needs to stay healthy. If your horse eats only hay cubes, he may need a daily multivitamin, which can be found at the feed store. Some owners feed their horses supplements to help specific body parts. For example, if your horse's hooves are crumbly, you could add to his diet biotin, a vitamin that strengthens hooves. If his coat is dull, supplements are available to make it shine.

Many owners feed their older arthritic horses supplements that include joint lubricants such glucosamine hydrochlo-

Left: *A racehorse needs a different diet than a child's pony.*
Above: *Check out the different feeds and supplements at a feed store.*

ride, chondroitin sulfate, or hyaluronic acid. Ask your veterinarian if she thinks a joint supplement would benefit your horse. When a supplement is required, simply mix it into your horse's meal. If your horse is fussy about what he eats, stir in some applesauce to hide the taste of the supplement.

TREATS

Apples and carrots are excellent treats for a horse and they are great for his digestion. Cut apples into quarters and carrots into finger-sized segments to make them easy for your horse to chew. Smaller pieces can get stuck in his throat and choke him.

Other special horse treats are available at feed stores, like cookies made especially for horses. Look for treats made with natural ingredients, such as oats or bran. Avoid giving your horse candy or sugar cubes because they aren't good for his teeth. It's best to feed treats in a bucket because feeding by hand can encourage nipping. Your horse might bite you if you don't have a treat for him.

WEIGHT WATCHING

Is your horse too fat or too thin? Either situation can become a problem: Being too fat can cause laminitis and leg strains, while being too skinny can make him less energetic. Wrap a weight tape around his girth area, just behind the withers, to estimate his approximate weight. A body condition score card (available at tack shops) will help you figure out if your horse is too thin or too fat.

Keep an eye on your horse's physical appearance. If he has a big belly, he may be too fat. If you can run your hands over his ribs but can't feel them, he's probably carrying too much weight. An overweight horse's neck appears bulgy and thick. If you can clearly see all of your horse's ribs or if his hipbones stick out, he's too thin. A skinny horse has a dent on either side of his tail on his hindquarters and his neck looks thin and weak.

Above: *If your horse starts biting, don't feed him treats by hand.*
Right: *Use a tape to figure out your pony's approximate weight.*

TOO FAT

If your horse is overweight, don't put him on a strict diet immediately—diet changes must be gradual. Instead, cut down the amount he eats over several weeks. If the feed you give him is 13 percent protein, try a mix with a lower percentage (less than 8 percent). Cut down on his hay intake. If he gets high-energy alfalfa, mix his ration with grass hay and gradually switch over to giving him only grass hay. Just like humans who are dieting, your horse needs regular exercise. Make sure he spends plenty of time out in a field (not a grassy one) so he can exercise.

If your field is full of green grass, put a grazing muzzle on him. This is a webbing mask that attaches to the halter. It has a small opening at the bottom so a horse can nibble on grass but not eat too much. If you use a webbing mask, don't keep it on your horse all the time, just during the day or at night. Make sure it fits properly and doesn't rub.

TOO THIN

If your horse is thin, deworm him immediately and put him on a regular deworming schedule. Get a horse dentist to float his teeth. To help your horse gain weight, give him as much good-quality hay as he'll eat. If he eats grass hay, switch him over to an alfalfa/grass mix. Buy a feed with a high-fat content (8 percent or higher). And, split his feed into three meals. Eating several times a day can help a horse gain weight. Some owners add half a cup of corn oil to each meal to help a horse put on the pounds.

An overweight pony should get regular exercise.

CHAPTER SIX

A GOOD FIT

You wouldn't feel very happy if you had to wear really tight jeans, would you? Well, it's the same for your horse. Her tack must fit her comfortably or she may become grumpy and not want to do her work. (You can tell she's unhappy if her tail swishes from side to side or if she bucks or rears. An unhappy horse certainly won't be in the mood to jump fences or hit the trails.) If your horse is uncomfortable in her tack, you're not going to have a good ride.

SADDLE FITTING

If the saddle doesn't fit your horse comfortably, she'll send you some signals. For instance, she may grind her teeth or flatten her ears when you put it on her back and fasten the girth. She may stiffen when you mount her and she won't be as forward-moving or graceful as she is in the field without the saddle. She may refuse to jump. If you're having some of these problems, check your saddle.

To check proper fit, put your saddle on your horse without a pad. Stand behind her on a bucket and look at the back of the saddle. If you have an English saddle, you should be able to see daylight when you look through the saddle's gullet (the thin gap under the saddle). The gullet should be wide enough to clear your horse's spine. If the saddle presses on her spine, it could cause back pain. When you sit in an English saddle, you should be able to fit three fingers between the pommel and your horse's withers; the same goes for the other end at the cantle. At the front, slide your fingers under the saddle on each side. If you can't do this, especially around the D-ring area, the saddle is too narrow and will pinch her. If you ride in a western saddle, you should be able to fit three fingers between the pommel and her withers.

Opposite: *Make sure your pony's tack fits her comfortably.*
Top: *Can you see light through the saddle's gullet?*
Bottom: *You should be able to fit three fingers between the pommel and the withers.*

Next look underneath your saddle. Are there lumps in the stuffing that put uneven pressure on your horse's back? You may need to take your saddle to a saddler and have it re-stuffed.

If you're buying a new or used saddle, go to a store that will let you take it home to try out on your horse. Your parents may have to buy the saddle with a credit card before the store will let you take it home. If it doesn't fit, you'll have to return it in perfect condition. Some tack shops will send a representative out to your barn to fit the saddle. A trainer or knowledgeable adult can also help. If the saddle looks like it fits, take a spin on it. If your horse acts comfortable, and is willing to do her work, the saddle probably fits fine.

A badly fitting saddle cannot be fixed by putting a fluffy pad underneath it. If a saddle doesn't fit, all the pads in the world won't make the saddle suitable for your horse. You can sometimes tell if a horse has worn an ill-fitting saddle in the past because a saddle that pinches a horse can leave permanent white spots around her withers.

GIRTH GALLS

You may have to try several different kinds of girths before you find one that fits your horse properly. A badly fitting girth causes sores around her elbows that take a long time to heal. If your horse gets girth galls, she'll need a few days off until the sores heal. In the meantime, you'll need to find another girth.

The best girths absorb sweat, are usually made of cotton, and are unlikely to rub. If you want to use a leather girth, put a fleece cover on it when you're not showing. This keeps your girth clean and helps to relieve pressure points and eliminate girth sores. Wash the cover after every ride—mud on the cover can cause rubs.

BRIDLES AND BITS

Use the mildest bit that you can. If your horse goes quietly in a snaffle, there's no need to use a Kimberwicke. If she's strong and you can't stop her in a snaffle, you may need to use a more severe bit, like a twisted snaffle. You may have to try several different bits before finding the perfect one. And, you might not use the same bit every time you ride. A simple snaffle might be fine for trail riding and dressage, but you may have to switch to a stronger bit when you jump or barrel race. (You must have soft hands when you use a more severe bit—do not yank on the bit.) Whichever bit you choose, make sure it fits your horse. The mouthpiece of the bit should stick out about a quarter of an inch from each side of her mouth. If it's too wide, it will slide around and bruise her mouth. If it's too small, it will pinch her lips and cheeks.

A lumpy saddle needs restuffing.

Some experienced horse people think that you should see two or three wrinkles in the skin around the corner of the horse's mouth and if you don't see any wrinkles, the bit may be too low. Start with two or three wrinkles and see how she behaves. Your horse may not like the constant pressure of the bit on her mouth and you may have to lower it slightly.

When you fit a bridle, keep a hole-punch handy, because you may need to make adjustments. If a bridle fits properly, you should be able to slide a finger under it, all around your horse's head. Check that the cavesson noseband lies about two fingers below your horse's cheekbone—the bone that juts out on the side of her face. You should be able to stick two fingers underneath the noseband. If the bridle is too tight, your horse may shake her head while you're riding. It's important to loosen a bridle that is too tight, because a tight bridle can interfere with the horse's breathing.

A browband isn't adjustable so be sure to buy the right size. It should lie just below the base of her ears without cutting into them and it should be big enough to allow the headpiece to lie comfortably behind her ears. And finally, you should be able to fit the width of four fingers between the throatlatch and your horse's jawbone.

Left: The cavesson should lie about two fingers under the cheekbone.
Top: The throatlatch shouldn't be tight.

GADGETS GALORE

Gadgets that control a horse's headset or the way she moves should not be found in your tack trunk. Avoid using items like draw reins, Market Harboroughs, or Chambons. Only experienced riders or trainers use these gadgets. They should not be used to fix problems you're having with your horse. If you don't know how to use these items properly, they can stress out your horse.

TACKING UP

To avoid possible mistakes, take your time when tacking up your horse. It's easy to forget to fasten a buckle, and you don't want your bridle to fall off once you're mounted.

Above: Young riders shouldn't rely on gadgets like side reins.
Right: Place the saddle gently on your pony's back.

Put the saddle on her back gently. Don't just throw it up and let it land—this hurts your horse's back. Place the saddle and pad slightly forward on her neck, then slide them back into place. This prevents hair from getting bunched up underneath the saddle.

Tighten the girth gradually—don't just yank it up in one go. Horses hate it when you tighten the girth too quickly and may act grumpy or try to nip you. Loosely fasten the girth, and then put on your horse's bridle. Go back to the girth and tighten it a bit. Put on your helmet, then tighten the girth some more. Just before you mount, tighten it one final time.

Be gentle when putting on your horse's bridle. Don't clank the metal bit against her teeth. If she doesn't open her mouth as the bit gets closer, stick your thumb into the side of her mouth to get her to open it. If it's difficult to put the bit on your horse, pour some molasses on it or rub some applesauce on it so that it tastes nicer. Be just as gentle taking the bit out of her mouth. Pull the headpiece over her ears slowly so she knows that the bit is going to come out. Wait until she opens her mouth, and then let the bit drop out. Don't bang it against her teeth or pull it out. In cold weather, warm the bit with your hands; if it's hot out, check that the sun hasn't heated your bit because it could burn your horse's mouth.

Above: *Tighten your horse's girth gradually.*
Right: *Let the bit drop out of your horse's mouth.*

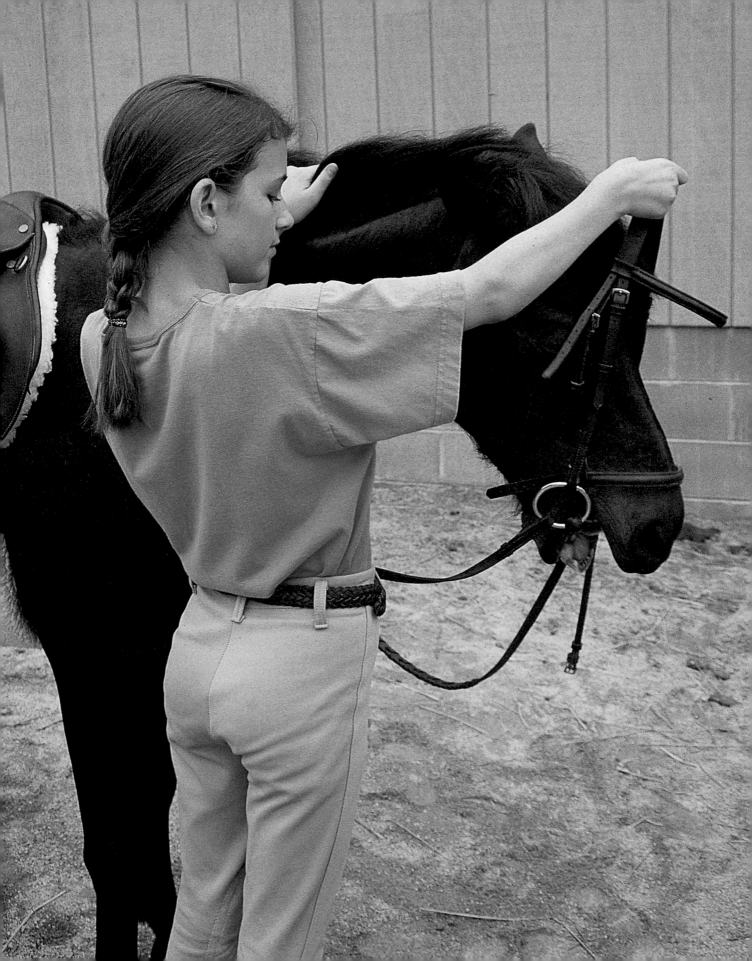

BLANKETS

Before buying a blanket for your horse, ask yourself, "Does she really need one?" Most horses can live quite happily without one because they adapt to colder temperatures by growing thicker coats. However, purebred horses like Arabians and Thoroughbreds have thin coats so they might need a blanket when it's chilly.

Blankets usually come in 2-inch increments. To figure out your horse's size, use a tape measure and start at the center of her chest, continuing around the widest part of her hindquarters to the middle of her tail. If your horse falls between sizes, go with the larger size. If a blanket is too big, it will rub off the hair on her neck and shoulders. Rubs happen quickly, yet it takes a long time for this hair to grow back. (Blankets with nylon lining rub less.) Once the blanket is on your horse, you should be able to fit your hand around the neck opening; it shouldn't be tight.

If your horse lives outside all the time and wears a blanket, visit her every day to make sure her blanket hasn't shifted. Sometimes, a blanket can slide to one side and scare the horse. If this happens, take off the blanket and make sure she's okay underneath it. It's a good idea to have two turnout blankets. That way, if one gets soaked in the rain it can be taken off and left to dry while she wears the second one.

Also, pay attention to the weather: if it's sunny and warm, take the blanket off.

If you don't ride a lot in the winter, your horse will probably be fine without a blanket. But if you ride almost every day, you'll find that a fuzzy horse gets sweaty and it takes a long time for her coat to dry. You won't want to turn her out while she's wet, nor will you want to hang around the stable for two hours waiting for her to dry. The solution may be to clip her. It's best to leave as much hair as you can on your horse in the winter, so a trace clip (which takes hair off her sides, belly, and underneath her neck) or a belly clip should be fine. Leave hair on her legs and head to keep her warm. Once you've clipped your horse, she'll need a blanket when she's in the stall and out in the field.

Left: *A clipped horse must wear a blanket.*
Above: *The blanket neck opening shouldn't be too snug.*

CHAPTER SEVEN

IN AND OUT OF THE SADDLE

There are lots of activities you can do with your horse, both in and out of the saddle, that can strengthen the bond between you. The more time you can spend with your horse the better. If your horse spends all his time munching on grass, he won't be in good shape to walk the trails or jump fences when you do decide to ride him.

ON THE GROUND

If your horse lives in a stall or a pen, one of the best things you can do with him is put on his halter and lead rope and take him out to graze in-hand on a patch of grass. Horses love to munch on grass—and you're helping his digestive system by letting him nibble on roughage. If you can, get your horse out at least once a day to graze. If your horse's field is bare, take him out to a different area of the boarding facility and let him have a 15-minute munch fest (get permission from your parents or the barn owner before doing this). Bring a soft brush with you and give him a quick grooming while he eats. The brush action massages him, and if you brush gently, he'll really enjoy it.

Spend time playing "games" with him on the ground. For information on horse games, check out the Parelli Natural Horsemanship program (www.parelli.com). The Parelli system teaches you and your horse how to play fun games that will help you later when you need to handle or ride him. For example, to play the "Friendly Game," touch your horse all over his body. This helps him get used to people touching and handling him, which comes in handy when the vet or farrier visits. The "Porcupine Game" teaches him valuable skills like "back up" or "move over." For another activity, put horse blankets or a plastic tarp down on the grass and lead your horse over them. He may sniff and snort a bit, but be patient and work with him until he follows you, walking quietly over the scary items without hesitation. Even though you'll play some of these games out of the saddle, they'll teach your horse skills that will help him on the trail or in the show ring.

Give your penned horse the chance to munch on grass.

FOLLOW THE LEADER

A horse who follows you anywhere, even if he's frightened, is worth his weight in gold because you never know when you might need him to follow you. This trust will come in handy when you're having fun, like jumping over a spooky ditch on a cross-country course, or in a more serious situation like a fire at the barn.

To train your horse to follow you, set up a few tiny fences in the arena, and then put on your helmet and gloves. You'll use the fences later. But first, grab a halter and a lead rope and walk your horse around the arena a few times to warm him up. After about ten minutes of walking and trotting, lead him at a trot on a loose lead rope over a small fence. Have him jump all of the fences this way. This exercise teaches your horse to jump without having you on his back, making him unbalanced. Raise the fences as he gets more confident. If your horse trusts you, he'll jump most things to keep up with you.

TRAILER TIME

A horse needs to know how to get in and out of a trailer. Even if you don't transport him much, he'll need practice getting in and out of a trailer for those emergency trips to the equine hospital. If your horse is used to following you around, he shouldn't be too worried about getting into a trailer. If he hasn't traveled much or if he's young, practice loading him into a trailer a couple times each month. Make it a stress-free activity that ends with him getting a tasty

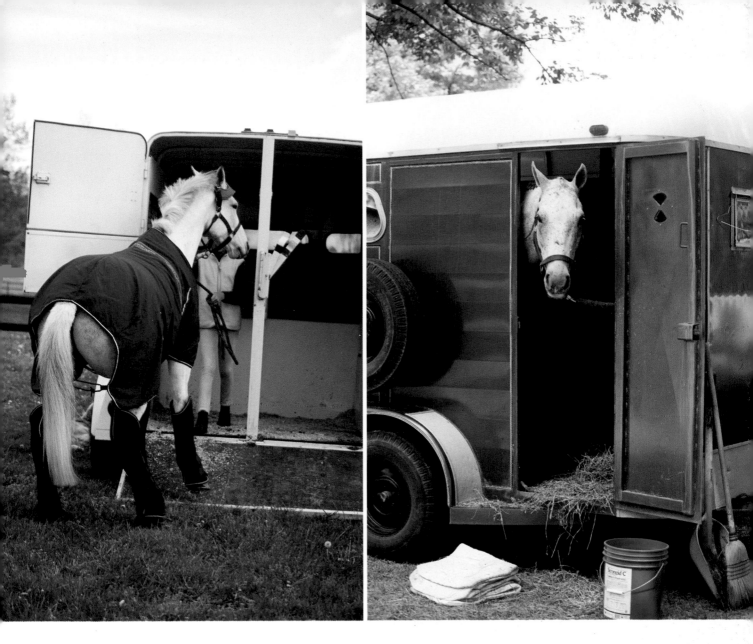

treat once he's loaded. Then, since he's used to the routine, he'll walk right into the trailer—no problem—when you really need to transport him.

If your horse is nervous at first, be patient. Swatting him with a whip might get him into the trailer once, but it won't teach him to load willingly. Instead tie him to the trailer and groom him. Get him used to being around the trailer. When you practice loading, ask an adult experienced in horses to help you. If you still have problems, check out videos by Pat Parelli or John Lyons. In both videos, the trainers demonstrate safe loading techniques; either video should help you with your horse.

Opposite: *Jumping together boosts your pony's confidence.*
Above Left: *Practice loading your horse into the trailer regularly.*
Above Right: *Being in a trailer shouldn't stress out your horse.*

FIT FOR FUN

If your horse huffs and puffs after trotting around the arena twice, he's probably not fit. He can't go to the gym or swim a few laps by himself, so it's up to you to be his exercise coach. If he spends most of his time outside in a field, then walking and running around with his field mates will give him enough exercise to trail ride once or twice a week. But, if you plan to jump him or do games, he'll have to be in better shape, because an unfit horse can easily strain a muscle and get hurt.

Be aware that getting your horse in shape takes longer than a day or two. In fact, it will probably take about five weeks to get him to peak fitness. Your first week of fitness training should be spent going on trail rides at a brisk walk. Keep your legs on your horse and ask him to keep moving along. If you don't have trails, walk around the fields of your boarding facility. Introduce hill work into the second week of your program. Walk him up and down the hills around your boarding facility. By the third week, you should be trotting and cantering as well as incorporating schooling sessions into your fitness program. By the fourth week, you can trot and canter for longer spells, and you can even practice jumping or barrel racing. By now, you should be sitting on a fit horse. It's time to check out show schedules and plan your competition schedule.

Opposite: *It can take several weeks to get your pony fit.*
Above Left: *It won't be long before your horse is in tip-top shape.*
Above Right: *Walking up and down hills improves your pony's stamina.*

SCHOOLING SESSIONS

It's important to have an arena (even a homemade one) for schooling your horse. Having boundaries helps you practice the moves you need at shows, like circles or straight lines. If you don't have an arena, make one in the field, using cinder blocks and wooden landscape poles from your local home improvement store. If you plan to do dressage tests at shows, your arena should measure 61 feet by 131 feet. You can do 20-meter circles (a good schooling exercise) in an arena this size.

Always warm up your horse before a schooling session. Go on a short trail ride or walk around the arena three or four times. These activities help to loosen up your horse's muscles and get him into a working mood.

Keep schooling sessions short and varied. Most horses get bored after about 25 minutes of work. Don't listen to people who brag, "My horse was so bad, I rode him for two hours until he got better." Riding a horse for hours might make him fitter, but it doesn't mean that he'll be more obedient the next time you ride. Drilling your horse over and over on the same move or pattern will make him sour and unwilling to work. So, after he's trotted nicely in several circles, move on to something else, for instance a serpentine. If you're not sure what to do when you school, take some riding lessons. A trainer

Make your own arena in a field.

can tell you what you need to work on when you're riding by yourself and can give you lessons to do with your horse. Take notes and carry them with you when you ride.

A NICE CHANGE

Think of different activities to do with your horse. For example, don't work him in the arena every day—how boring for both of you! Sure, you have to school a couple times a week, because it makes your horse more obedient and supple. But, as you know, too much schooling can be dull. If you have trails around your barn, saddle up your horse and go exploring with him. (Always take a friend with you in case something goes wrong.) If you don't have trails, ride around the fields. Being out in the open is exciting for your horse. If you have a trailer, take your horse somewhere different at least twice a month. Sign up for a lesson at another barn or go on a trail ride at a state park. Talk to your trainer or parents about other places to ride in your area. Be creative and have fun.

REGULAR RIDING LESSONS

If you always ride by yourself, it's easy to slip into bad habits. For example, you might not realize that your hands are moving up and down, causing your horse's head to bob around. Regular lessons with a good train-

er can help both you and your horse avoid such bad habits. If you can afford it, have a lesson at least twice a month.

Left: *Going on a trail ride is a nice change for your horse.*
Above: *Regular lessons improve your riding skills.*

83

If you're looking for a trainer, ask your friends for a recommendation. You want someone who is a good rider and is kind to horses. You don't want someone who is rough and uses gadgets on the horses she rides. Don't put up with a teacher who yells at her students—keep looking for another teacher.

When you do hear about a good trainer, watch her give a few lessons. Her classes should be small and everyone should get the same amount of attention. Her students should look confident and be having a good time. Most importantly, a good trainer should like your horse and treat him nicely. If she's mean to him or rides him roughly, find a different trainer.

THE PONY CLUB AND THE 4-H CLUB

You can have lots of fun with your horse by joining the United States Pony Club or the 4-H Club. Joining such a club gives you and your horse opportunities to ride in different places and do lots of awesome activities together.

The Pony Club teaches English riding and horse-management skills to young riders through the age of 21. You can learn how to look after your horse properly, try a new sport like eventing, or take part in special competitions. The Pony Club also holds instructional rallies and summer camps. Contact the USPC (www.ponyclub.org) to find the club nearest you.

Equestrian groups in the 4-H club hold instructional meetings and group rides for English, western, and saddle seat riding. 4-H club members learn horse-care skills and participate in horse shows. 4-H clubs usually hold summer camps, too. 4-H clubs are organized in almost every town across America. To join your local 4-H, look up the local Cooperative Extension office in your telephone book under County Government or go to the club's Web site (www.4h-usa.org).

Above: *Demonstrate your horsey knowledge at Pony Club rallies.*
Right: *4-H clubs hold fun horse shows.*

CHAPTER EIGHT

WHEN GOOD HORSES GO BAD

If you spend lots of time around horses, you've probably noticed that a few of them have a quirk or two. Some have vices—annoying habits—while others are more interested in eating grass than jumping fences. Just like humans, each horse has her own special personality. Sadly, humans cause most horsey problems. Why? Because we make horses live in unnatural environments and ask them to do things they normally wouldn't do. For example, if given a choice, your horse wouldn't sleep in a stall and she probably wouldn't jump a three-foot fence with you on her back.

Instead of allowing horses to spend time in a field grazing, we box them into small stalls or pens where they get little exercise. And then, guess what? They get bored! And boredom leads to vices. Wild horses *never* develop vices. So, let your horse live as natural a life as possible—she should be outside in a field most of the time—and she'll probably stay vice free. Let's take a look at some problems and what you can do to solve them.

CRIBBING

When a horse grabs an object, usually wooden, and pulls up and back with an arching movement of the neck, she is cribbing. Cribbing makes a horse feel good because it causes her brain to release endorphins, natural substances that produce a happy feeling. This is why horses like to crib. But, cribbing can ruin fences, barns, and trees in no time at all.

Left: *Horses who live outside most of the time rarely develop vices.*
Above: *A cribber can ruin wooden fences.*

87

cribbers. Now, animal behaviorists believe that, while some foals may learn this behavior from their moms, a horse is unlikely to pick up the habit when she's older—even if she shares a field with a cribber. Studies show that most cribbers spent a lot of time in stalls when they were younger and began cribbing to replace grazing.

To stop cribbing, some people put special muzzles on their horses, enabling them to graze, but keeping them from grabbing wood with their mouths. You can also place a well-fitting cribbing collar on your horse, but when you take it off, she's likely to crib again. To make sure that your young horse doesn't start cribbing, allow her to spend as much time as she can outdoors.

WEAVING

Weaving is another habit caused by a horse spending too much time in a stall. You can tell if your horse is weaving if she stands in front of her stall door or window and rocks back and forth on her front legs. Nervousness or excess energy can also cause weaving, conditions that are easily cured with plenty of free time out in a field.

Once a horse picks up a weaving habit, it's hard to break her of it. She'll waste a lot of energy rocking and may lose weight. You can hang tires or water-filled plastic bottles from the ceiling in the doorway, but constant weavers will just bump into these items and continue their strange dance.

Years ago people thought horses learned how to crib by watching other horses, so owners kept their horses away from

Above: A cribber may have to wear an anti-cribbing collar.
Right: If your horse is nibbling on wood, give her more hay.

WOOD CHEWING

Wood chewing is different than cribbing. A wood chewer simply gnaws on wooden fences, feeders, and stall walls. These are signs that she's not getting enough roughage or is missing a certain mineral in her diet. To stop the excess chewing, put a mineral block for her to lick in her field and add more hay to her daily diet. You can also put a grazing muzzle on her or paint the tops of the fences and other chewable surfaces with a bad-tasting anti-chew product available at any feed store.

MOODY MARES

If you're lucky, you may not be able to tell when your mare is in heat (ready to mate).

But, sometimes, a mare can be sensitive when she's in heat. She may be extra-ticklish or act grumpy when you groom her or tack her up. She may be frisky in the field and want to hang around other horses. A quiet mare may act up in the ring or out on a trail.

Most mares come into heat in late spring and summer, and their cycle may last anywhere from a few days to three weeks. If you can't ride your horse when she's in heat because her behavior is unpredictable, your veterinarian may be able to prescribe a hormone-suppressant drug for her. Your horse should be back to her old self within a few days.

HAZARDOUS HORSES

If you've got a horse-behavior problem that could harm you—and if it seems to be getting worse—don't try to solve the problem by yourself. Get help quickly from a trainer or vet. Then, if you still can't stop your horse's naughty behavior, you might need to sell her to someone who can deal with her problems.

Riding is supposed to be fun, and if your horse kicks you or dumps you every time you ride her, it might be time for a change. There are plenty of good horses in the world and there's one out there just waiting for you to find her. Here are some other problems you might face when you ride and take care of horses:

Biting: Biting is often a result of hand-feeding your horse her treats. A horse who is hand-fed tidbits regularly starts to expect them, so if you come to her without one, she might bite you. To avoid this bad habit, feed your horse treats in a bucket. Also, without holding any treats, spend time stroking her and rubbing your hands around her nose and muzzle area, so she gets used to your hands around her face.

Young horses often bite in fun. They are used to nipping their pals as part of their playtime. But they need to learn that they can't nip at people. If your young horse nips, tie her up on a short line so she can't turn around and nip you. If your horse tries to bite you, tap her on the nose and say "No!" in a firm voice. Then go back to whatever you were doing.

Kicking: If you own a kicker, it's best to let an adult discipline her because when a horse kicks she must be punished immediately. Carry a crop around her, and if she strikes out at you, smack her on the hindquarters right away with the crop.

Left: *If your horse bites, feed her treats in a bucket.*
Above: *Warn others that your horse kicks by putting a red ribbon on her tail.*

If she kicks out while you're grooming, you might be tickling her. Brush her lightly and be gentle around the sensitive areas of her body. If she kicks another horse while you're riding her, use your crop to swat her on her hindquarters immediately so she knows that she's being punished for kicking. Tie a red ribbon to her tail to alert others that your horse is a kicker and to stay away. Even if your horse is not a kicker, be aware of other horses with red ribbons and keep your horse away from them.

Bucking: High spirits or a badly fitting tack usually cause bucking, but naughtiness can also be a cause. Check your horse's saddle and make sure it fits properly, and get the veterinarian to look at her. (She might be bucking because she has a sore back.) If the saddle fits and nothing is wrong with her, study her diet. Is she getting too much high-energy food and not enough exercise? (Kids can become hyperactive if they eat too much candy.)

The most important thing to do when riding a bucking bronco is to keep her head up and to keep her moving forward. If a horse is moving, it's difficult for her to buck.

If you feel a buck coming on, shorten your reins and kick your horse to make her walk forward briskly. Pick up the trot and school her in circles so she's got something to concentrate on and she forgets about bucking.

Rearing: Rearing is extremely dangerous because a horse can tip over backwards and fall on her rider. Your horse can't rear if she's moving forward, so keep her moving. This is especially important if you're in a situation where you think she might rear. For instance, you might worry that your horse will rear at the arena gate during a show. If she starts to rear in this situation, and you can't move her forward, tap her behind your leg with a whip.

If your horse does rear, loosen the reins and lean forward. Wrap your arms around her neck. Don't pull back on the reins because you'll cause her to be unbalanced and she might fall over. If she starts falling backward while you're riding her, drop your stirrups and bail out. Try to fall to the side so she doesn't fall on top of you. If your horse rears a lot, a trainer needs to work with her. But keep in mind: a rearing horse doesn't make a good horse for a child. If the rearing problem continues, sell your horse to a more experienced rider—one who can handle this dangerous habit.

Bolting: Your horse may run off with you when she's frightened or when she's going fast and gets excited. You must stop her because she might trip in a hole or run into a fence, hurting both of you. The first thing you must do is circle, circle, and circle some more. Shorten one rein and physically pull your horse's head toward your knee. She can't run if she's circling, so she'll have to slow down.

If you don't keep a bucker's head up, you could end up on the ground—ouch!

If your horse is a bolter, don't ride with a loose rein. Keep enough contact so that you can stop her quickly if she takes off at top speed. You may need to use a stronger bit so that when you pull on the reins, she'll pay attention to your hands. If you ride her in a plain snaffle, you may have to switch to a twisted snaffle or a Kimberwicke.

TOUGH DECISIONS

Hopefully, your horse doesn't have any of these problems, but if she does, you must take action and try to solve them. You might be able to stop some bad habits, like kicking. Others, like cribbing, you'll have to learn to live with. (Cribbing won't prevent your horse from winning ribbons.) But if a problem is really serious, like rearing, talk to your parents and trainer about it. A badly behaved horse may hurt you—even if she doesn't do it on purpose.

If you don't enjoy riding your horse you must admit it to yourself. Not every horse and human is a perfect match. Toughen up and sell your horse to an experienced horse person who can work with her to improve her behavior.

Above left: A bolting horse might step into a hole or run into something.
Above right: Turn a bolting pony into a tight circle.
Right: Ask a trainer for help with a tough pony.

CHAPTER NINE

SAYING GOOD-BYE

Riding is supposed to be fun. If you're getting dumped by your horse or you're afraid to take him out of the arena, it's time to think about getting a new four-legged friend. It can be hard to admit that your horse isn't right for you because even the naughtiest horse is lovable sometimes. But your horse must be suitable for your riding level. Know when you'd be better off with a quieter horse. If your horse is too much for you to handle, you won't have fun riding. If you can't stop your horse or ride him outside the arena, you'll never go trail riding or experience show events.

If your trainer thinks that you should sell your horse, listen to her. A good trainer wants you to have a safe, happy riding partnership with your horse. She wants you to become a better rider and you won't improve if you're scared. A good trainer will help you sell your horse and look for another one that will better suit your needs.

The decision to sell your horse may have less to do with his behavior and more to do with his ability. If you dream of leaping over fences, but your horse hates to jump, he'd be better off with a dressage rider. If you want to barrel race, but your horse is slow, he'd be happier with someone who wants to trail ride.

Left: *Riding your pony should be great fun.*
Above: *Falling off all the time can damage your confidence.*

HORSE FOR SALE

It's really sad when you must sell a horse, but there are ways to make the break up less painful. If you know that he's going to a good home, you won't feel as bad about saying good-bye. As his owner, it's your responsibility, along with your parents and trainer, to make sure he goes to a caring, knowledgeable rider.

It's important to be careful when deciding who will buy your horse. An experienced horse is likely to go to a good home with a family who will look after him properly. But, if your horse isn't an expensive purebred that jumps hunter courses beautifully, he may end up in an unsuitable place.

When selling your horse, first tell your horse friends and local Pony Club and 4-H leaders that he's for sale. Put an ad in the newspaper or place signs at nearby tack shops. When people call, tell them all about your horse. Be honest—you want to find him a great home. If you say he can jump three-foot fences, but he can barely stumble over trotting poles, the new owners probably won't keep him for long.

Left: *An experienced horse can usually find a good home.*
Above: *Tell all of your pals that your pony is for sale*

When a young rider tries your horse, find out how she wants to ride him. If she wants to jump, let her pop him over a few fences. You'll be able to tell if the rider clicks with him or not. If you like the rider, ask her parents where they'll be keeping the horse and if a trainer will be helping them. If they can't answer your questions, they probably won't be good owners. Some buyers may invite you to look at their farm or boarding facility so you can feel comfortable about selling your precious horse to them. As a horse owner, it should be your number one goal to find a good, stable home for your horse—a place where the next young rider will love him as much as you do.

AUCTIONS

An auction is not a good method of finding a new home for your horse, unless a breed association, like the Pony of the Americas Club, is sponsoring it. If you sell your horse at an auction, you'll have no idea where he'll end up going. There are almost always people at small auctions who are willing to take horses home, fatten them up, and then sell them to the slaughterhouse.

OTHER OPTIONS

If money is not an issue with your family, here are some other ideas for you to consider:

Donate Your Horse: Many handicapped-riding programs accept donated horses and ponies who are well behaved and quiet. An older horse is often perfect for one of these programs. Your horse will have to go to the program's facility for a trial run. If he doesn't behave well, he'll be returned to you. If he stays, he'll be well cared for. To check if there is a program near you, go to the North American Riding for the Handicapped Web site at www.narha.org.

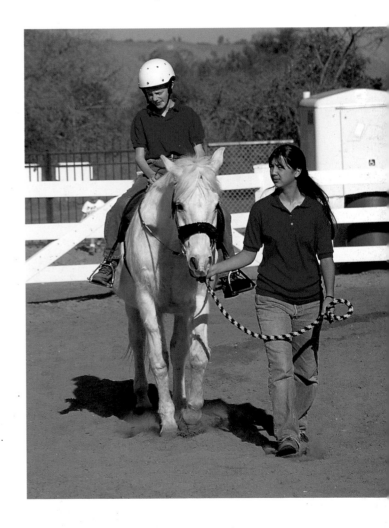

Left: *Get to know your horse's new owner before you hand him over.*
Above: *Donate your quiet horse to a riding for the handicapped program*

Give Away Your Horse: This can be risky for your horse so before giving away your horse, you should know something about the people as well as something about their home. Remember, too, that these new owners may be planning to sell him or give him away shortly after taking him from you. So hand him over with the provision that he is returned to you if they can't keep him.

Also, beware that sometimes shady people will take a horse, saying that he'll be for their kid. Then they'll take the horse to an auction, sell him, and pocket the money. Be sure to involve your parents or trainer in figuring out the best option for your horse's new home.

TOO BIG FOR YOUR PONY?

All kids grow, and if you have a pony, you're eventually going to get too big for him. What will you do? If you're a responsible pony owner you'll make sure that, even if you've outgrown him, the rest of his life is a healthy and happy one. Let's look at some of your options if you've outgrown your pony.

Keep Your Pony: If you live on a farm, you may be able to offer your pony a home for life. He can be a companion to other horses or there might be a smaller child in your town who can ride and care for him. You could buy an inexpensive jog cart and teach him how to drive—you might even be able to enter a driving competition someday!

Above: *Make sure you are actually giving your horse to a young rider.*
Right: *Ponies are great companions.*

Loan or Lease Your Pony: You can "loan" or "lease" your pony to someone who will board him somewhere and pay for all of his expenses, including vet care and feeding. Leasing means that someone pays you money to borrow your pony. Loaning means he's free. In both cases, you'll still own your pony, but someone else will care for him.

It's best to loan your pony locally so that you can check up on him and see him at 4-H shows or Pony Club rallies. If you find a potential rider for him:

- check out the farm where he'll live;
- watch the child ride him;
- make sure the child's parents know how to look after a pony;
- meet the child's trainer;
- have both parties sign a lease on the pony (a trainer will have a contract you can use);
- and be prepared to take your pony back if things don't work out.

Left: *Try to loan your horse to a child with horsey parents.*
Above: *If you loan your pony to a local rider, you may see him at shows.*

STAY IN TOUCH

It's always nice to know what's going on with your horse after you've sold him. Exchange addresses with the people who buy him and ask them to keep in touch with you. Remember, you have no control over what happens to your horse once you've cashed the buyer's check. This is why it's important to make sure the new owners know how to care for a horse and get along with your horse. This is not a responsibility that should fall on a young person, so involve your parents or trainers when selling your horse.

READING AND RIDING

If you want to be a good friend to your precious horse, you need to be an educated owner. Grab every horsey book you can get your hands on. Check them out of the library or buy them at the local tack shop or bookstore. Reading books like this one boosts your horsey knowledge. The other kids at the barn will wonder how you got so smart!

But more importantly, with a little equine knowledge under your belt, you'll be able to see if your horse is sick and you'll know when it's important to call the vet right away. You'll be able to look after him with your first aid kit if he gets injured. You'll understand how he thinks and why he acts the way he does. And, you'll let him live the most "natural" life possible. Enjoy your happy and healthy horse. You're going to have loads of fun handling and riding him.

Left: *It's great to visit your pony in his new wonderful home.*
Above: *Keep in touch with the rider who has bought your pony.*

USEFUL ADDRESSES

American Association of Equine Practitioners
4075 Iron Works Parkway
Lexington, KY 40511
859-233-0147
www.aaep.org

American Association for Horsemanship Safety
P.O. Box 39
Fentress, TX 78622
512-488-2220
www.horsemanshipsafety.com

American Connemara Pony Society
2360 Hunting Ridge Road
Winchester, VA 22603
540-662-5953
www.acps.org

American Farrier's Association
4059 Iron Works Parkway
Lexington, KY 40511
859-233-7411
www.americanfarriers.org

American Horse Council
1616 H Street NW
7th Floor, Washington,
DC 20006-3805
202-296-4031
www.horsecouncil.org

American Miniature Horse Association
5601 South Interstate 35W
Alvarado, TX 76009
817-783-5600
www.amha.org

American Morgan Horse Association
P.O. Box 960
Shelburne, VT 05482
802-985-4944
www.morganhorse.com

American Paint Horse Association
P.O. Box 961023
Fort Worth, TX 76161
817-439-3400
www.apha.com

American Quarter Horse Association
P.O. Box 200
Amarillo, TX 79168
1-800-414-RIDE
www.aqha.com

American Riding Instructors Association
28801 Trenton Court
Bonita Springs, FL 34134
293-948-3232
www.riding-instructor.com

American Youth Horse Council
577 North Boyero Avenue
Pueblo West, CO 81007
800-879-2942
www.ayhc.com

Appaloosa Horse Club, Inc.
2720 West Pullman Road
Moscow, ID 83843
208-882-5578
www.appaloosa.com

Arabian Horse America
12000 Zuni Street
Westminster, CO 80234
1-877-551-2722
www.arabianhorseamerica.com

Canadian Pony Club
Box 127
Baldur, Manitoba ROK OBO
1-888-286-PONY
www.canadianponyclub.org

CANTER—The Communication
Alliance to Network
Thoroughbred Ex-Racehorses
10801 Last Drive
Plymouth, MI 48170
734-455-0639
www.canterusa.org

CHA—The Association
for Horsemanship Safety
and Education
5318 Old Bullard Road
Tyler, TX 75703
800-399-0138
www.cha-ahse.org

Future Farmers of America
P.O. Box 68960
Indianapolis, IN 46268-0960
317-802-6060
www.ffa.org

Intercollegiate Horse
Show Association
P.O. Box 741
Stony Brook, NY 11790
516-751-2803
www.ihsa.com

The Jockey Club
821 Corporate Drive
Lexington, KY 40503
859-224-2700
www.jockeyclub.com

National 4-H Council
7100 Connecticut Avenue
Chevy Chase, MD 20815
301-961-2830
www.fourhcouncil.edu

North American Riding
for the Handicapped
Association
P.O. Box 33150
Denver, CO 80233
800-369-RIDE
www.narha.org

Parelli Natural
Horsemanship
P.O. Box 3729
Pagosa Springs, CO 81147
800-642-3335
www.parelli.com

Pony of the Americas Club
5240 Elmwood Avenue
Indianapolis, IN
46203-5990
317-788-0107
www.poac.org

The United States
Pony Club
4041 Iron Works Parkway
Lexington, KY 40511
859-254-PONY
www.ponyclub.org

Welsh Pony and
Cob Society of America
P.O. Box 2977
Winchester, VA 22604-2977
540-667-6195
www.welshpony.org

USA Equestrian
4047 Iron Works Parkway
Lexington, KY 40511
859-258-2472
www.equestrian.org

Young Rider Magazine
P.O. Box 8237
Lexington, KY 40533
859-260-9800
www.youngrider.com

GLOSSARY

banking: using bedding to create a bank around the edges of a stall to prevent a horse from lying too close to the wall and getting stuck

belly clip: trimming the coat underneath a horse's belly

bit: the mouthpiece on a bridle

bridle: a head harness used to control and guide a horse when riding or driving

canter: a three-beat gait resembling a slow gallop

cantle: the rear part of the saddle that slopes upward

cavesson noseband: a noseband that runs between the bit and the beginning of the cheekbones

Chambons: a headsetting device that encourages the horse to lower his head and neck; should only be used by a knowledgeable person

colic: a painful stomach illness that can be fatal

cribbing: an undesirable habit in which a horse bites or chews the wood of a stall or fence

crop: a short riding whip with a looped lash

curry comb: a grooming tool used to remove dirt from a horse's coat

draw reins: reins that run from the girth area through the rings of a snaffle bit to the rider's hands

dressage: training a horse on the flat to perform movements and exercises in a supple, obedient manner. Also, a sophisticated form of riding in which the horse performs difficult steps in a balanced manner

hand: a 4-inch measurement used to measure horses from the ground to the withers

farrier: a person who shoes horses and trims their hooves

floating: to file down irregular teeth for a better chewing surface; rasping

gallop: a fast 4-beat gait of a horse

gelding: a male horse who has been neutered

girth: a band that encircles a horse's belly to hold a saddle

girth galls: sores around the girth area caused by excessive pressure or friction

grade horse: a mixed breed

grazing mask: a webbing mask that attaches to the halter and prevents a horse from eating too much grass

gullet: the thin gap under the saddle

Gymkhana events: a riding meet with informal contests on horseback

halter: a head harness without a bit made out of leather or nylon

Kimberwicke bit: a bit that has a low port or snaffle, short cheek pieces, and curb chain

laminitis: inflammation of soft tissue in the foot

mare: a female horse

Market Harboroughs: a headsetting device that runs from the girth to the bit which prevents a horse from lifting his head up and evading the bit

muck: bedding that has been soiled by manure and urine

noseband: a strap of leather that goes around a horse's nose

Palomino: a golden colored horse with a blonde mane and tail

pipe corrals: a horse pen made of metal pipes

pommel: the arched front of the saddle

rearing: to raise up on hind legs

schooling: warming up or training a horse

snaffle bit: type of bit with a straight or jointed mouthpiece

tack: saddle, bridle, and other equipment used in riding and handling a horse

trace clip: the partial clipping of a horse, leaving the full coat on the top part of the body and lower part of the legs

trot: a natural two-beat gait in which the forefoot and diagonally opposite hind foot strike the ground simultaneously

weaving: an undesirable habit in which a horse sways back and forth in a compulsive manner in his stall

withers: the ridge between the shoulder bones of a horse

worming: to treat an animal for parasitic worms